3x
————
8/06   10/06

D0624616

ALSO BY ANITA DOREEN DIGGS

SUCCESS AT WORK: A GUIDE FOR AFRICAN AMERICANS

STAYING MARRIED: A GUIDE FOR AFRICAN AMERICAN COUPLES

BARRIER-BREAKING RÉSUMÉS AND INTERVIEWS

BARRIER-BREAKING

RÉSUMÉS AND

INTERVIEWS

JUMPING THE HURDLE
OF UNEMPLOYMENT
AND GETTING A JOB

ANITA DOREEN DIGGS

TIMES **T** BOOKS

RANDOM HOUSE

Library of Congress Cataloging-in-Publication Data

Diggs, Anita Doreen.
    Barrier-breaking résumés and interviews : jumping the hurdle of
unemployment and getting a job / Anita Doreen Diggs. — 1st ed.
        p.   cm.
    ISBN 0-8129-3130-0 (alk. paper)
    1. Résumés (Employment)   2. Employment interviewing.   3. Job
hunting.   I. Title.
HF5383.D48   1999
650.14—dc21   99-14789

Printed in the United States of America on acid-free paper
Random House website address: www.atrandom.com

98765432
First Edition

BOOK DESIGN BY CINDY LA BREACHT

THIS BOOK is dedicated to all of the inmates being released today, to all of the public assistance recipients being thrown off the rolls today, and to everyone else struggling to make it in a society where the gulf between the haves and have-nots continues to grow wider by the minute.

ACKNOWLEDGMENTS

FIRST I WANT TO THANK my editor, Manie Barron, who made the writing, rewriting, and polishing process a whole lot of fun in spite of the fact that at one point I had almost turned him into a life counselor. He bore the burden with wit, wisdom, and kindness. Such is the editor/writer relationship at times!

Recognition must be given to Adrienne Ingrum, who came up with the idea for this book and had faith in my ability to write it.

Thanks, as always, to my mother, brother, daughter, aunts, uncles, and cousins. I love you all.

TABLE OF CONTENTS

INTRODUCTION

BARRIER-BREAKING RÉSUMÉS AND INTERVIEWS is not an ordinary how-to-find-a-job book. This book is for those who have little or no work experience, have just been released from jail, or were formerly on public assistance.

If you fit into one of these categories, this book will teach you how to figure out what kind of job to look for, who to call or write to, and what to say when you meet them.

City, state, and federal agencies are putting a lot of pressure on businesses to hire ex-offenders and people who have been forced off the welfare rolls. Although some of these businesses are patient with individuals who have little or no work experience, most expect everyone they hire to show up with a decent work ethic and good social skills the first day on the job.

Barrier-Breaking Résumés and Interviews will give you a head start.

—Anita Doreen Diggs
August 1999

BARRIER-BREAKING RÉSUMÉS AND INTERVIEWS

CHAPTER ONE

GETTING A JOB

LEROY GOT OUT OF JAIL six months ago. He moved in with his sister, her husband, and their five children. Since the family didn't have an extra bedroom, Leroy slept on the pullout couch in the living room and kept his clothes in a box in the corner.

Every morning for a month, Leroy got up early and walked around the neighborhood to small grocery stores, asking for work. The answer was always the same. "Sorry, we don't need any help." After four weeks of getting turned down, Leroy gave up. "There ain't no jobs out there," he said.

Leroy was wrong. People like him get hired for new jobs every day. The difference between those who get hired and those who don't is simple: Those who get work understand how to job-hunt, have the right tools, and know how to use them.

Before we go into detail about these three necessary steps to becoming employed, let's talk about one very important matter. In order to get a job, you must have something definite to offer the person who is in a position to hire you. Which of the following job hunters would you hire?

JOB HUNTER #1: Good morning. My name is John Doe, and I'm looking for a job.

MANAGER: Glad to meet you, Mr. Doe. What kind of work do you do?

JOB HUNTER #1: Uh . . . I dunno. I can do anything if I put my mind to it. Just tell me what y'all do here and that's it.

OR

JOB HUNTER #2: Good morning. My name is John Doe, and I'm here to apply for the file clerk job you have open.

MANAGER: Glad to meet you, Mr. Doe. Have a seat.

JOB HUNTER #2: Thank you. Here is my résumé. As you can see, I filed papers in the principal's office all through high school.

Which person would you hire? Job Hunter #2, of course! He came in knowing what he wanted, with proof that he could do the job. More on this in Chapter Seven.

WHAT KIND OF JOB IS RIGHT FOR YOU?

If the sound of children running, jumping, playing, and making loud noises makes you want to scream, then a job in child care isn't right for you.

If you would be afraid to walk up to people and demand that they empty their pockets so you can check for stolen items, you would make a terrible security guard.

If your friends and neighbors are always asking you to do their hair, and you enjoy it, why not train to be a hairdresser?

There are thousands of different jobs, from apple picker to zoologist, but we are going to keep things simple and only talk about twenty-two.

JOB:	**ADMINISTRATIVE ASSISTANT**
WHAT THEY DO:	Performs a variety of secretarial duties, such as typing reports and memos, maintaining computer-based and paper files, answering office inquiries, and handling special projects of a moderate to highly skilled nature
TRAINING NEEDED:	High school diploma and three years' secretarial experience
WHERE THEY WORK:	A variety of offices, from one-person establishments to multinational corporations

JOB: BUSBOY

WHAT THEY DO: Performs maintenance duties so that cooks and waitresses can work in a clean, safe environment

TRAINING NEEDED: None

WHERE THEY WORK: Restaurants

JOB: CABLE TV INSTALLER

WHAT THEY DO: Visits homes by appointment and installs boxes that allow residents to receive nonnetwork TV programs

TRAINING NEEDED: Each company has its own training program with different requirements

WHERE THEY WORK: Cable service providers

JOB: CUSTOMER SERVICE REPRESENTATIVE

WHAT THEY DO: Responds to service requests, inquiries, and complaints over the phone or in person; adjusts complaints and ensures maximum good will from transactions

TRAINING NEEDED: High school diploma and 1–2 years' sales or service experience

WHERE THEY WORK: Telephone services, mail-order houses, computer companies, large retail stores, credit-card firms

JOB:	**FACTORY WORKER**
WHAT THEY DO:	Generally assembles products in a manner prescribed by the company
TRAINING NEEDED:	On-the-job training provided
WHERE THEY WORK:	Factories

JOB:	**HAIRDRESSER**
WHAT THEY DO:	Washes, conditions, perms, colors, cuts, and styles hair according to customer desires
TRAINING NEEDED:	Cosmetology license
WHERE THEY WORK:	Beauty salons, barber shops, spas, department stores, nursing homes

JOB:	**MEDICAL TECHNICIAN**
WHAT THEY DO:	Draws blood samples and performs other duties as directed by doctors and nurses
TRAINING NEEDED:	Trade school
WHERE THEY WORK:	Clinics, hospitals, and private laboratories

JOB:	**MAILROOM CLERK**
WHAT THEY DO:	Performs routine tasks, including receiving, sorting, and delivering the mail; distributes and collects department mail; may maintain records on postage, registration of mail, and packages
TRAINING NEEDED:	On-the-job training provided
WHERE THEY WORK:	Large companies in every industry

JOB:	**MANICURIST**
WHAT THEY DO:	Fingernail maintenance and styling
TRAINING NEEDED:	Cosmetology license
WHERE THEY WORK:	Beauty salons, barber shops, spas, department stores, nursing homes

JOB:	**MAINTENANCE WORKER**
WHAT THEY DO:	Works under direction of a building superintendent to make small repairs, paint, and improve apartment units
WHERE THEY WORK:	Apartment buildings

JOB:	**MESSENGER**
WHAT THEY DO:	Delivers letters and packages by foot, bicycle, public transit, or car
TRAINING NEEDED:	None
WHERE THEY WORK:	Large corporations and private messenger companies

JOB:	**NURSE'S AIDE**
WHAT THEY DO:	Assists nurses in all phases of patient care
TRAINING NEEDED:	Trade school
WHERE THEY WORK:	Clinics and hospitals

JOB:	**RECEPTIONIST**
WHAT THEY DO:	Meets and greets visitors; answers telephones; occasionally types correspondence
TRAINING NEEDED:	Secretarial course to learn software programs and office procedures; requires patience, excellent appearance, verbal skills, and pleasant disposition
WHERE THEY WORK:	Small, medium, and large companies in all industries

JOB:	**SALES CLERK**
WHAT THEY DO:	Helps customers find specific items, explains store policies, and describes goods being sold
TRAINING NEEDED:	Each retailer has its own training program
WHERE THEY WORK:	Boutiques, shoe stores, department stores, record shops; generally, anyplace where merchandise is displayed for sale
JOB:	**SECRETARY**
WHAT THEY DO:	Types reports, answers phones, schedules appointments, types correspondence
TRAINING NEEDED:	Secretarial course to learn software programs and office procedures
WHERE THEY WORK:	Small and large companies in industries of all types
JOB:	**SECURITY GUARD**
WHAT THEY DO:	Protects property against fire, theft, and illegal entry; makes routine periodic tours around buildings and grounds; checks visitors for proper identification and clearance
TRAINING NEEDED:	None unless a firearm is necessary, in which case, a state-issued gun permit is required
WHERE THEY WORK:	Stores, banks, office buildings, apartment buildings, warehouses

JOB: **SHIPPING AND RECEIVING CLERK**

WHAT THEY DO: Compares contents of material being received or shipped to records of contents requested; follows established procedures to report discrepancies

TRAINING NEEDED: On-the-job training provided

WHERE THEY WORK: Shipping department of retail stores, warehouses, factories

JOB: **SUPERINTENDENT**

WHAT THEY DO: Provides maintenance, minor repairs, and improvements to units of housing when not otherwise provided by building management, e.g., repairing plumbing, moving furniture, changing lightbulbs, plastering, and painting; cleans and disinfects all new apartments and existing units before new occupancy

TRAINING NEEDED: Must possess good organization skills and be able to work independently; high school diploma or GED, maintenance experience required.

WHERE THEY WORK: Building and housing complexes

JOB:	**SUPPLY CLERK**
WHAT THEY DO:	Orders office supplies and keeps them stocked in an orderly manner; distributes materials to staff as needed and keeps accurate records
TRAINING NEEDED:	Basic reading and math ability, high school diploma or GED required
WHERE THEY WORK:	Large corporations

JOB:	**TRUCK DRIVER**
WHAT THEY DO:	Hauls goods from one organization to another
TRAINING NEEDED:	Commercial driver's license required
WHERE THEY WORK:	Local and long distance firms

JOB:	**TV/VCR REPAIRMAN**
WHAT THEY DO:	Fixes broken television sets and videocassette recorders
TRAINING NEEDED:	Some electrical background desired: trade school course or previous jobs
WHERE THEY WORK:	Repair shops and retail stores that service appliances sold there

JOB:	WAITRESS/WAITER
WHAT THEY DO:	Takes customer orders, brings food and beverages, clears tables
TRAINING NEEDED:	Pleasant disposition
WHERE THEY WORK:	Small and large restaurants

WHO ARE YOU?

To figure out which job to go after, you have to be honest with yourself about who you really are and what you like to do.

THE TOOLS YOU NEED FOR A JOB HUNT

➤ COVER LETTER

➤ RÉSUMÉ

➤ REFERENCE

COVER LETTER—A cover letter is used to introduce you, highlight important parts of your résumé, and request an interview (see page 54).

RÉSUMÉ—A résumé (pronounced **REZ-OO-MAY**) tells the employer where you've worked, what education and skills you have, and where you can be reached.

Both cover letters and résumés must be typed and each one should not be longer than a page. We will talk more about résumés and cover letters, as well as look at samples, in Chapter Three.

REFERENCE—A reference is the name, address, and phone number of a person who knows how well you work and is willing to say good things about you if he or she is contacted. A reference can be a former teacher, a counselor, a former employer, a church pastor, or a friend with a good reputation. Most companies will ask for three references before offering you a job.

HOW TO FIND OUT ABOUT JOB OPENINGS

There are many ways to find out what companies are looking for someone to do the kind of job you'd like to do:

1. Ask friends and relatives to let you know if they learn of an opening at their company or anywhere else.

2. If you are on parole, ask your parole officer to help you find work.

3. If you are on public assistance and need to get off, ask your caseworker to recommend you for job placement programs.

4. Visit community organizations and ask if they can help.

5. Register with employment agencies, which usually run ads in the Help Wanted section of your daily newspaper, and fall into two categories: companies that help you find

permanent jobs, or those that specialize in locating temporary positions. (See "Employment Agencies and How to Handle Them," page 17.)

6. Look in the Help Wanted section of your daily newspaper and circle all the jobs that are right for you. To answer an ad, send a cover letter and résumé. Remember to keep your letter short and point out that you have the skills they are looking for. All you want is an interview.

7. Using your local yellow pages, make a list of every company that you would like to work for. If you live in a big city like New York, Los Angeles, or Chicago, there should be at least 100 company names on the list by the time you finish. Call each company and find out the name of the person who does the hiring for the type of job you want. Send that person a cover letter and résumé.

8. Register at your local unemployment office. Make sure to bring a résumé with you.

9. Visit the local cultural organizations (Sons of Vietnam Veterans, Puerto Rican Pride Society, etc.) and ask them for help. Make sure to bring a résumé with you.

10. Check the bulletin boards at every library in your city. They usually carry news of job fairs and notices of city and state job tests.

CLASSIFIED ADS AND HOW TO READ THEM

When companies place Help Wanted advertisements in newspapers, they are charged by the number of letters or space they use, so they try to squeeze a lot of information into a small space by abbreviating.

Take a look at this ad, which is designed to take up very little space and save money for the company.

Secretary
Exp'd req'd. F/T. Fax res to: (212) 733-0071

What they really mean is:

We need a full time secretary with experience. All résumés should be sent by fax machine to: (212) 733-0071

Here is a list of codes. Use it when you're searching for a job in the Help Wanted section of the newspaper.

CODE	MEANING
+	Plus
Bnfts	Benefits
EOE	Equal Opportunity Employer
Eqpmt	Equipment
Exc	Excellent
Exp'd	Experienced
Fee Paid	Agency pays fee to the company
Flex	Flexible
F/T	Full-time
Hrs	Hours
Immed	Immediate
Indivs	Individuals

K	Thousand
Loc	Location
Mjr	Major
Oppty	Opportunity
PC	Personal Computer
Perm	Permanent
Pref	Preferred
Prof'l	Professional
P/T	Part-time
Rep	Representative
Req'd	Required
Res	Résumé
Temp	Temporary
W/	With
Wk	Week
Yr	Year

When you answer an ad, keep your cover letter short. Don't give away too much. Just get two points across: (1) I have the skills you need, and (2) I'll contact you again for an interview.

EMPLOYMENT AGENCIES AND HOW TO HANDLE THEM

An employment agency is a company that finds workers to fill job openings for their clients. Their clients may be warehouses, law offices, or clothing stores, to name a few. Whether you are looking for work as a secretary, warehouse laborer, or restaurant help, there is an employment agency that handles workers of that type.

Some agencies place workers in permanent jobs. Others deal in temporary jobs that can last from a day to a couple of months. Although some agencies charge a fee to find you a job, most of them do not, and you should stick with those that get paid by their client and not you, the worker. If it's not in the ad, ask to make sure they are a fee-paid agency.

No matter what type of agency you walk into, the procedure will usually go something like this:

➤ The receptionist will give you an application to fill out.
➤ You will be tested on any type of office equipment you say you can use.
➤ Someone will interview you.
➤ The agency will keep your name and skills on file and phone you each time they get a call for someone who fits your description.

The best way to help an agency remember you is to ask for the interviewer's business card and make a polite phone call once every two weeks. Register with at least a dozen agencies for best results.

WHEN IT ALL BECOMES TOO MUCH

If you're doing everything we've discussed in this chapter, you will be spending 25–30 hours a week on your job hunt. It may be that you have a caseworker or parole officer pressing you to hurry up and find something, or family members who are unwilling or unable to keep helping you out with carfare, food, and a place to stay. Whatever the case, sooner or later you may start to feel pressure from somebody. Don't give up. Don't lose hope. Try to find another way to solve the problem.

For instance, if you can't find one good full-time job, take two part-time jobs until you can do better.

Make sure you're going after companies of all sizes. In other words, if you're looking for a job as a busboy, there should be large restaurants, medium-sized restaurants, soup and sandwich shops, and even tiny coffee shops on your list.

Form a club with at least three other people who are in the same position you're in. Meet once a week and trade ideas, talk about your problems, and help each other. Most important of all, the four of you must talk about all the job openings you know about but that you are not right for. Chances are, someone else in the club will fit the bill.

If the club doesn't work for you and there is still no job in sight, ask your parole officer or caseworker to help you get professional help dealing with your anger or depression before your emotions get out of control.

Always remember that if you absolutely refuse to give up, eventually someone will hire you.

CHAPTER TWO

RULES FOR REVELATION

ROSA GONZALEZ WORKED VERY HARD in high school and graduated at the top of her class. She married right away. That was eight years ago. Rosa and her husband had four children before he lost his job and the marriage fell apart. Rosa was forced to go on welfare. Now that her youngest child is in school, she wants a job, but no one will hire her because she has no work experience. "How can I write a résumé when there is nothing to put on it?" she asks.

When Rosa was in high school, she tutored other students in math, organized school trips, was president of the glee club, and ran for class president. Since then, Rosa has been the leader of her daughter's brownie troop, helped raise money for her church, and participated in a community action group to rid her neighborhood of drug dealers. Rosa was not paid for doing any of those things, but that doesn't matter. It all added up to a really great résumé (see page 34).

ANY WORK EXPERIENCE CAN GO ON A RÉSUMÉ, WHETHER YOU GOT PAID FOR IT OR NOT.

Sharon had a different problem. She spent six years in prison for drug dealing, but she put those years to good use. While doing her time, Sharon learned typing, word processing, and data entry, and worked three days a week in the warden's office, so she started her job hunt with excellent skills and six years of solid work experience. Although Sharon sent out dozens of résumés, no one ever called her for an interview. "It's because they're afraid to hire somebody who just got out of jail," she says bitterly.

Sharon made a big mistake by revealing her problems with the law on her résumé. True, you cannot hide your past from an employer, but the place to discuss it is at the interview, not on the résumé.

THE PURPOSE OF COVER LETTERS AND RÉSUMÉS IS TO GET YOU IN THE DOOR FOR AN INTERVIEW.

Creating a good résumé starts with one basic rule: There are some details about your life that you MUST list and other things that you NEVER include. What you MUST include:

1. **YOUR FIRST AND LAST NAME.** Do not include nicknames. Even if everyone from your mama to your counselor calls you "Sonny" or "Tee-boy," these words should not appear anywhere on your résumé.

   There is no need to write Mr., Ms., or Mrs. in front of your name unless your first name could belong to a man or a woman, as with "Jordan" or "Leslie." In that case, it is okay to write Mr. Leslie Jones or Ms. Jordan White.

2. **YOUR ADDRESS.** Here is the correct way to write it:

   Mr. Leslie Jones
   457 West Park Place, Apartment 2R
   New York, NY 10000

   Make sure this is a place where you can pick up your mail every single day. If a friend is letting you use his or her address but will be away, find someone else to do you the favor. Do not call someone you want to work for and say something like "I was just checking cuz my mail goes to Pookie's house and he ain't home."

3. **YOUR TELEPHONE NUMBER.** If people want you to come in for an interview, they will probably not send you a letter. Instead, they will pick up the phone and call you. Make sure that if you are using someone else's number, that person knows about your plans and can talk to callers in a professional manner. Don't let something like this happen:

   EMPLOYER: May I speak to Leslie Jones, please?

   PHONE OWNER: Who?

EMPLOYER:	Mr. Leslie Jones left this number when he applied for a job.
PHONE OWNER:	A job? Oh, yeah, you must mean Tee-boy . . . well, he got a whole lotta nerve givin' out my number just cuz I let him sleep on the couch one night. Hold on.

[*Phone owner drops the phone with a loud thunk and yells "Yo, Tee-boy" through the house, then returns to the phone.*]

PHONE OWNER:	He ain't here. Can you call back?

How many of you readers honestly believe that the employer will call back?

4. **JOB OBJECTIVE.** This one is easy. The job objective simply explains what kind of job you're looking for. For example:

JOB OBJECTIVE:	Telephone operator

5. **WORK EXPERIENCE.** Here is where you list the work you've done in the past. Make sure to include unpaid work, community service, or anything that shows an employer that you can take on a task and complete it in a responsible manner.

6. **EDUCATION.** Your educational record is ordinarily mentioned, although where it is placed depends on where you stand in life. If you got out of school a short while ago and have no work experience, your education is the best thing you've got going for you, and should appear near the

beginning of your résumé. If you went to college, put that before high school even if you did not receive your college degree.

ITEMS THAT ARE ABSOLUTELY NEVER PLACED ON A RÉSUMÉ

➤ THE REASON WHY YOU LEFT A JOB. SAVE YOUR EXPLANATIONS FOR THE INTERVIEW AND THEN **ONLY IF ASKED.**

➤ THE NAME OF A PRISON.

➤ LIES.

➤ ANYTHING THAT WILL INDICATE YOUR POLITICAL BELIEFS.

➤ THE NAMES OF THE PEOPLE YOU PLAN TO USE AS REFERENCES.

➤ THE SALARY YOU ARE LOOKING FOR.

And this brings us to the gatekeeper, a very important person in the world of job hunting.

WHO IS THE GATEKEEPER?

The word "gatekeeper" is slang for the receptionist or secretary who can keep you from getting through the "gate" and into his or her boss's office for an interview. Gatekeepers are usually the people who open the mail, which means they are the first people to read your cover letter and résumé and decide whether to let them get past the "gate" and onto the interviewer's desk or to file them away without ever letting the interviewer get a look.

HOW THE GATEKEEPER MAKES THE DECISION—Lorna Feldman works in the human resources office of a large New York hospital. She says, "The first person to touch the résumé takes a pencil and highlights key words that determine the applicant's experience and education. He or she checks the résumé for grammar and spelling errors. Résumés that don't indicate the right education or experience are screened out. He or she then gives the other résumés to the person doing the hiring, the decision maker."

THE DECISION MAKER

Once the interviewer gets a pile of good résumés, he or she will decide which people to interview. Although it is illegal to deny someone an interview because of their race, it is probably done all the time. How would you know? Since the purpose of the résumé is to get you an interview, do not write anything on the résumé that gives away the fact that you are a minority, if you can help it (exceptions to this rule are discussed in Chapter Three). Lorna Feldman also brings up another important point. "Avoid controversial issues as well. If an applicant's résumé says 'Attended Million Man March,' that might be seen as problematic whether the interviewer is white or black."

BARRIER-BREAKING RÉSUMÉS AND COVER LETTERS

THE RÉSUMÉ IS NOT a place for you to tell the story of your whole life—just your work life. It should be short, which means one page, and again, never put the salary you are looking for on your résumé.

There are many different types of résumés, but we will focus on the chronological résumé and the skills résumé.

A chronological résumé is used by people without gaps in their employment history.

Use a skills résumé if there have been periods of unemployment in your life due to incarceration, public assistance, or other issues.

Some of the résumés which follow are in the chronological format; the others use the skills format. Choose the type which fits your life situation.

THERESA WILLIAMS
50 East 65th Street
Chicago, IL 30011
(312) 123-4567

Job Objective   Administrative Assistant for large real estate firm

Experience   King Realty Inc.
Jan. 1994 to   Executive Secretary
Present

➤ Prepare monthly reports

➤ Do light bookkeeping

➤ Keep track of tenant rent payments

➤ File leases

➤ Type correspondence

Dec. 1992 to   Majestic Realty Inc.
Jan. 1994   Secretary

➤ Answered phones

➤ Typed correspondence

➤ Opened mail

➤ Scheduled appointments

Education   George Hays High School, Chicago, IL: December 1993

References   Available upon request

GLENN ANDERSON
7500 Western Avenue
Los Angeles, CA 90600
(213) 123-4567

Summary of Background

Worked in a large institution for five years handling a large volume of soiled cooking and eating utensils.

Experience

➤ Cleared tables

➤ Stacked pots, pans, dishes

➤ Ran dishwasher

➤ Cleaned institutional kitchen and returned clean pots, pans, dishes to their proper places

Education

GED, State of California, 1992

References

Available upon request

ROY BARNES
1900 West Street NW
Washington, DC 20001
(202) 123-4567

Job Objective   Cable TV Installer

Experience   Indianapolis Cable TV
Oct. 1993 to   Cable TV Installer
Nov. 1995
➤ Installed cable boxes on television sets in residences and office buildings

➤ Kept records of all jobs

➤ Filed leases

➤ Followed up on television inquiries

May 1991 to   Indianapolis Cable TV
Oct. 1993   Assistant Cable TV Installer

➤ Accompanied Senior Installer and assisted on installation jobs

➤ Set up new accounts

➤ Kept records for main office

Education   AAS, Electrical Engineering
Cable County Community College, 1991

References   Available upon request

DONALD CARLSON
501 Ledge Drive
Albany, GA 32715
(912) 123-4567

Job Objective	Car mechanic for large, well-established shop
Experience March 1995 to May 1998	Joe's Autobody Car Mechanic ➤ Checked gas and oil ➤ Repaired heating and air-conditioning ➤ Tuned-up engines ➤ Serviced brake lines
Aug. 1994 to June 1995	Ted's Buff & Shine Auto Assistant ➤ Washed automobile interiors ➤ Wiped excess suds from automobile exteriors ➤ Collected money from customers ➤ Swept inside office ➤ Wore sandwich board to advertise company
Dec. 1985 to Aug. 1994	The Car Place Car Mechanic ➤ Maintained engine performance ➤ Checked gas and oil ➤ Replaced shock absorbers ➤ Cleaned cars
Education	Albany High School, Albany, GA: 1985
References	Available upon request

ARLENE YANCY
1624 Harden Road
Columbia, SC 29200
(803) 123-4567

Job Objective	Cashier in Diner
Experience Oct. 1997 to Present	Larry's Burger Barn Cashier ➤ Light record keeping ➤ Collect money and process customer credit cards
Jan. 1995 to Oct. 1997	Betty's Diner Cashier ➤ Collected money and processed customer credit cards ➤ Waited tables during heavy traffic
Education	Received GED, State of South Carolina, June 1994
References	Available upon request

CAROL WALKER
552 Bishop Road
Little Rock, AR 72200
(501) 123-4567

Job Objective Day-care Assistant

Experience Just Like Home, Inc.
July 1995 to Day-care Assistant
Aug. 1998
➤ Served breakfast and lunch to 3-year-olds

➤ Played games with 4-year-olds

Sept. 1992 to Mama's Den
July 1995 Clerk

➤ Answered phones

➤ Filed children's activity sheets, lesson plans, and medical records

➤ Processed parent applications

➤ Purchased games for preschoolers

Education Received GED, State of Arkansas, June 1995

References Available upon request

ROSA GONZALEZ
109-15 167th Avenue
Jamaica, NY 11422
(718) 123-4567

Summary of Background

Have worked as a volunteer in various neighborhood projects for the past eight years.

Experience

- ➤ Fundraiser for Jamaica Christ Church
- ➤ Leader of Jamaica Girl Scout Troop #513
- ➤ Field Worker at Coalition for a Drug-Free Community

Education

Brandeis High School: Peer-tutored math students, organized school trips, served as glee club president. Received academic diploma with high honors, 1991.

References

Available upon request

WILLIAM PAULSON
145 Barr Avenue West
Raleigh, NC 28075
(919) 123-4567

Job Objective   Customer Service Representative

Experience   Raleigh Phone Company
Oct. 1994 to   Customer Service Representative
Dec. 1995
➤ Answered questions

➤ Managed three phone lines

➤ Processed bills and payments

➤ Completed questionnaires regarding type and length
   of calls received

➤ Prepared and sent customer surveys

➤ Mailed brochures describing new phone company
   services

➤ Explained telephone features to new customers

Education   Raleigh High School, Raleigh, NC: 1990

References   Available upon request

NELSON HILL
2316 East Street
Baltimore, MD 21211
(410) 123-4567

Summary of Background

Worked in a large institution for fifteen years producing license plates and other products for use by general public.

Experience

➤ Pressed license plates

➤ Supervised workers in assembly-line atmosphere

➤ Counted supplies

➤ Handled paperwork related to volume and distribution

Education

Working toward GED

References

Available upon request

LADONNA PATRICK
1995 Gentilly Street
New Orleans, LA 70120
(504) 123-4567

Summary of Background

For many years, I have washed, conditioned, dyed, permed, braided, and straightened hair for my friends, neighbors, and associates.

Experience

➤ Worked in beauty salon of large institution for twelve years

Education

Cosmetologist License, Louisiana State: 1998

New Hills High School, Baton Rouge, LA: 1980

References

Available upon request

MARTIN BASE
1200 18th Avenue East
Nashville, TN 37200
(615) 123-4567

Job Objective   Lab technician for large hospital

Experience   Nashville Women's Center
June 1989 to   X-ray Technician
June 1997

➤ Prepare monthly reports

➤ Light bookkeeping

➤ Keep track of tenant rent payments

➤ File leases

➤ Type correspondence

Education   Blake Trade School, June 1996–June 1997
Completed one-year course; skills learned include
administering EKG and drawing blood

References   Available upon request

LYLE CHARSON
750 View Ridge Lane
Atlanta, GA 30300
(404) 123-4567

Job Objective Mailroom clerk for large corporation

Experience Gordon Films, Inc.
Sept. 1997 to Mail Clerk
Present

➤ Process incoming and outgoing mail

➤ Run xerox machine

➤ Operate color duplicator

Aug. 1996 to Sweet Pea Drugstore
Sept. 1997

➤ Stocked shelves

➤ Swept floors

➤ Ran errands

Education Atlanta High School, Atlanta, GA: May 1996

References Available upon request

STANLEY WALL
2280 Simpson Road
Dallas, TX 75240
(214) 123-4567

Summary of Background

Have worked as building superintendent for landlord of twelve-family tenement apartment building for six years.

Experience

- ➤ Plastering
- ➤ Painting
- ➤ Minor repairs
- ➤ Waste removal

Education

Attended Dallas High School 1950–1953

References

Available upon request

ANNIE WOODARD
2310 Corprew Avenue
Norfolk, VA 25300
(804) 123-4567

Summary of Background

Since high school I have placed small ads in neighborhood newspapers and charged for nail care, which I learned in my senior year.

Experience

➤ Clip and buff nails

➤ Polish nails

➤ Design nail tips

➤ Handle wedding parties from 5 to 20

Education

Working toward Virginia State cosmetology license

Lincoln Vocational High School, Richmond, VA: June 1993

References

Available upon request

ROWLAND WOODRUFF
2100 Cleburne Street
Houston, TX 77000
(713) 123-4567

Summary of Background

Worked as a messenger for Woodruff Lawn Service during all four years of high school.

Experience

➤ Picking up letters and packages

➤ Delivering letters and packages

➤ Answering phones

Education

Willis High School, Houston, TX: June 1999

References

Available upon request

PHYLLIS DOLD
1400 North Lombardy Street
Richmond, VA 23200
(804) 123-4567

Job Objective	Nurse's Aide
Experience July 1998 to May 1999	Richmond Realty, Inc. Secretary

➤ Answered phones

➤ Filed

➤ Typed correspondence

➤ Assisted tenants of condominium with filing requests for change in rules

➤ Paged maintenance workers to handle repairs

Education	Richmond Trade School: completed 300-hour course in patient care and efficient methods of assisting nurses
	Richmond High School, Richmond, VA: June 1998
References	Available upon request

KAREN GREENE
612 17th Street, Apt. 6C
Oakland, CA 94600
(510) 123-4567

Job Objective   Receptionist

Experience   Oakland Community College
Sept. 1996 to   Receptionist, Admissions Office
Present

➤ Field student inquiries

➤ Receive and direct heavy volume of phone calls

➤ Type correspondence

➤ File

Sept. 1994 to   Law Offices of Hill & Sanders, LLC
Sept. 1996   Receptionist

➤ Met and greeted clients

➤ Kept attorney's appointment calendar

➤ Answered phones

Education   AAS Secretarial Science, 1997
Oakland Community College

Oakland High School, Oakland, CA: 1994

References   Available upon request

LAWRENCE HOPE
9 Greenwich Avenue
New York, NY 10014
(212) 123-4567

Job Objective   Sales Clerk

Experience   The Wiz
Christmas 1996   Sales Assistant

- ➤ Helped customers find merchandise
- ➤ Carried heavy appliances to register for customers
- ➤ Fielded inquiries regarding prices and availability
- ➤ Relieved gift wrapper during lunch breaks

Summer 1997   Woolworth's
Stock Boy

- ➤ Stacked shelves
- ➤ Swept floors
- ➤ Removed damaged merchandise from inventory

Education   Stuyvesant High School, New York, NY: 1996–Present

References   Available upon request

PATRICIA A. DANIELS
100 West 125th Street
New York, NY 10025
(212) 123-4567

Job Objective   Secretarial Position

Work Experience   JVZ Corporation, New York, NY
August 1997   Responsibilities and duties include:
to Present

➤ Open and process mail

➤ Type correspondence

➤ Answer phones

➤ Greet visitors

August 1996 to   Lilyput Ltd., Houston, TX
August 1997   Responsibilities and duties included:

➤ Typing correspondence

➤ Reception duties

➤ Handling phones

➤ Making travel arrangements

Education   GED, State of New York, May 1994

Office Skills   Microsoft Word 4.0

References   Furnished upon request

JULIA WHEELER
730 East 56th Road
Chicago, IL 60630
(312) 123-4567

Summary of Background

Have volunteered for security duty at college dorms, summer camps, and school trips; have escorted visiting church dignitaries around Chicago.

Experience

➤ Checked bags for unauthorized items

➤ Sat guard duty in hallway of women's dormitory during special events

➤ Guided groups of fifty or more schoolchildren on long-distance trips

Education

Working toward GED from State of Illinois

References

Available upon request

CARL HUNTER
17203 Gilbert Avenue
Cincinnati, OH 45201
(513) 123-4567

Summary of Background

Sole person responsible for shipping and receiving cartons for a medium-sized organization.

Experience

➤ Checked bills of lading against supervisor's requisitions

➤ Packed and taped boxes for pickup by UPS

➤ Carried boxes to appropriate locations and unloaded them

Education

Bayton High School, Cincinnati, OH: June 1989

References

Available upon request

LEO MOSLEY
9272 Miles Park
Cleveland, OH 44100
(216) 123-4567

Summary of Background

Worked as building superintendent for thirty-firm office building in New York.

Experience

➤ Had responsibility for ten skilled and semiskilled maintenance workers and janitors

➤ Hired outside help (plumbers, electricians, etc.) frequently to troubleshoot situations

➤ Position required excellent interpersonal and problem-solving skills

Education

Charles Evans Hughes High School, New York, NY: 1973

References

Available upon request

ROBERT KING
144 West 145th Street
New York, NY 10027
(212) 123-4567

Summary of Background

I have six years experience working in the supply room of a major corporation.

Experience

➤ Assisted colleagues in filling out supply request forms

➤ Maintained up-to-date records and compiled monthly inventory records

➤ Answered employee questions regarding availability of supplies

Education

GED, State of New York, 1975

References

Available upon request

SIDNEY BORDEN
1080 Bergen Street
Newark, NJ 07113
(201) 123-4567

Job Objective   Long-distance truck driver

Experience   NYNEX
Sept. 1982 to   Van Driver
Jan. 1994
➤ Drove small vehicle carrying supplies and telephone
   installation personnel

➤ Kept records of time and routes

➤ Collected paperwork from telephone installers on
   services performed

Education   Jersey City Community College
                     AAS Business Administration, 1982

                     Newark High School, Newark, NJ: 1980

References   Available upon request

STEVE FRAZIER
13205 Dexter Street
Detroit, MI 48248
(313) 123-4567

Summary of Background

Reliable and handy with tools of trade. Excellent interpersonal skills and record-keeping ability.

Experience

➤ 1986–1990 Owner/Operator Steve's TV & VCR repair

➤ Organized and established own business

➤ Sold services of shop to neighborhood clientele

➤ Trained other TV and VCR repair personnel

Education

GED, State of Michigan, 1984

References

Available upon request

DEBORAH H. MOORE
630 Second Avenue
Daytona Beach, FL 32115
(904) 123-4567

Job Objective   Waitress

Experience   The Daytona Luncheonette
May 1997 to   Waitress
Present
➤ Take meal orders

➤ Explain menu items to customers

➤ Work with chef to ensure smooth meal experience for customers

➤ Write bills

➤ Collect money and credit cards

Summer 1996   Daytona High School Cafeteria
                         Cafeteria aide

➤ Served meals at after-school program for elementary school students

➤ Kept order in the lunchroom

➤ Cleared tables after students departed

Education   Daytona High School, Daytona Beach, FL: May 1997

References   Available upon request

COVER LETTERS

It is worth repeating here that the job of a cover letter and résumé is to get your foot in the door for an interview. The cover letter goes on top of the résumé, so it is the first piece of paper that the company sees: In other words, it is the company's first impression of you.

A résumé lacking a cover letter very seldom captures the attention of an employer, and usually gets thrown away. I think that your cover letter has about five seconds to grab the interest of someone in a hiring position. Even a really terrific cover letter doesn't get more than five minutes of the person's time, so it makes sense to put some time and thought into writing yours.

The cover letter should include your name, address, and phone number at the top, and must be addressed to a specific person. Never send out a letter addressed "To Whom It May Concern." If you don't care enough to find out who that person is, why should the employer care enough to pick up the phone and call you?

The cover letter must grab the employer's attention in the first sentence and explain what you want. It must also briefly mention a skill or attitude you have that will be useful to the company. Don't use the cover letter to explain why you've been out of work so long or why you left other jobs. If the employer wants that information, he or she can ask you at the interview. Remember, this is not your life story. Make the letter quick, quiet, and professional.

Keep the cover letter to one page. If it is longer than that, the reader will become impatient and wonder if you understand the realities of the work world.

A well-written cover letter makes the reader look forward to examining your résumé.

Here are eight sample cover letters for you to work with.

STEVE FRAZIER
13205 Dexter Street
Detroit, MI 48248
(313) 123-4567

(DATE)

Mr. Joe Billings
Owner
Joe Boy TV Shop
1 General Road
Detroit, MI 48200

Dear Mr. Billings:

Enclosed is a copy of my résumé in response to your advertisement in the February 3, 1999 issue of the *Free Press.*

I am a hard worker with four years' experience in TV repair.

I will call you next week to talk further.

Very truly yours,

Steve Frazier

enclosure

ROBERT KING
144 West 145th Street
New York, NY 10027
(212) 123-4567

(DATE)

Ms. Denise Mack
Director, Corporate Services
Mega International, Inc.
550 West 46th Street
New York, NY 10036

Dear Ms. Mack:

Per yesterday's conversation, I am forwarding a copy of my résumé to you.

I look forward to meeting you soon to discuss the secretarial opening.

Sincerely,

Robert King

enclosure

PATRICIA A. DANIELS
100 West 125th Street
New York, NY 10025
(212) 123-4567

(DATE)

Mr. Walter Gazek
Manager
ABC Insurance Company
1230 West 3rd Street
New York, NY 10004

Dear Mr. Gazek:

I am writing in response to your advertisement in the *Daily News* for a secretary. I have two years of secretarial experience and excellent skills. Enclosed is my résumé.

I will call you next week in the hope of setting up an interview.

Very truly yours,

Patricia A. Daniels

enclosure

LAWRENCE HOPE
9 Greenwich Avenue
New York, NY 10014
(212) 123-4567

(DATE)

Mr. Bob Kreg
Modern Retail Outlet
350 Hudson Street
New York, NY 10014

Dear Mr. Kreg:

As you requested in our telephone conversation this morning, I am enclosing a copy of my résumé for your review.

As you can see from my résumé, I have retail store experience and attend one of the most intellectually challenging high schools in the city.

I look forward to hearing from you soon.

Sincerely,

Lawrence Hope

enclosure

ANNIE WOODWARD
2310 Corprew Avenue
Norfolk, VA 25300
(804) 123-4567

(DATE)

Ms. Barbara Bergstrom
Barb's Beauty Barn
1 Anyplace Road
Norfolk, VA 25300

Dear Ms. Bergstrom:

As per my telephone conversation with Suzie of your beauty parlor yesterday, enclosed is my résumé.

I look forward to discussing the Manicurist opening with you shortly.

Very truly yours,

Annie Woodard

enclosure

LYLE CHARSON
750 View Ridge Lane
Atlanta, GA 30300
(404) 123-4567

(DATE)

Mr. Randall Pregny
Mailroom Manager
One Vieme Road
Atlanta, GA 30311

Dear Mr. Pregny:

I received your name from Mr. Sebastian last week. I had a conversation with him about the mail clerk opening in your department.

I would very much like to discuss the opening with you and enclose my résumé for your consideration.

Sincerely,

Lyle Charson

enclosure

NELSON HILL
2316 East Street
Baltimore, MD 21211
(410) 123-4567

(DATE)

Mr. Abe Lansfield
Lansfield Toy Company
One Any Street
Baltimore, MD 21200

Dear Mr. Lansfield:

I believe the fifteen years that I have spent in an assembly-line/
production-oriented environment may be of interest to you.

I will call you next week to discuss the opening you have for a factory
worker. In the meantime, I enclose my résumé for your review.

Sincerely,

Nelson Hill

enclosure

CAROL WALKER
552 Bishop Road
Little Rock, AR 72200
(501) 123-4567

(DATE)

Ms. Sheilah Sweete
Owner
Sweete Day Care Center
650 Boston Road
Little Rock, AR 72211

Dear Ms. Sweete:

I have three years' experience working with small children in a day-care setting. In addition, I am a very patient person with a warm and kind manner. Children like me.

I would welcome the opportunity to meet with you personally to discuss the opening at Sweete Day Care Center.

I will call you next week to set up an appointment.

Very truly yours,

Carol Walker

CHAPTER FOUR

PHONE ETHICS

LET'S TALK ABOUT the telephone. Although you're accustomed to using the phone to call your friends and relatives, business phone manners are a skill that must be learned.

There are at least three important types of calls that you will use during the job hunt.

CALL #1: To collect information about job openings and the people who hire for them

CALL #2: To set up or confirm an interview

CALL #3: To follow up once the interview is over

As you can see, trying to find a job without using the phone is like trying to drive a car that has no wheels. It can't be done. After you have settled on a phone number, make sure that the number will be answered at all times either by a human being or an answering machine. It is silly to work hard trying to find a job if you are going to miss important phone calls.

➤ Make sure you are ready for the phone call. Write down what you want to say so you don't get nervous and forget all the important things.
➤ When talking on the phone, sound like you have confidence in yourself, speak clearly, and don't use slang.
➤ Don't chew gum or have music or household noise going on in the background.

The first person you will usually come into contact with when you call a company is the receptionist. If you don't handle this conversation well, it will be difficult to get a chance to speak to the person in a position to hire you.

Receptionists say that the callers who commonly turn them off:

1. are inarticulate.

2. have bad diction.

3. behave in a pushy manner.

4. ask them to do too much.

5. ask salary questions right away.

What does all this mean?

1. **INARTICULATE.**—A person who is inarticulate does not clearly communicate, and as a result, the person on the other end of the line has no idea what the call is really about.

2. **BAD DICTION**—This can mean using improper English, slang, or both.

3. **PUSHY MANNER**—Some people try to get the receptionist to reveal more information than the company allows, or refuse to accept answers given to them. These are just two examples of pushiness.

4. **ASK THEM TO DO TOO MUCH**—One receptionist interviewed for this book says that job applicants frequently ask her to take their number and call them back when their boss comes in, or tell them who the firm's competitors are. This is not a receptionist's job.

5. **ASK SALARY QUESTIONS RIGHT AWAY**—It is a mistake to start talking about money before you even bother to find out what a job consists of, or whether the firm is interested in you.

Pay attention to why you're calling. Focus on the task at hand and make sure you have a solid idea of what you want the outcome to be before you pick up the phone. If you get nervous making calls, use an index card to write down all your points before the call and check them off as you go along.

Come across as very human and warm on the phone. One way to do this is to keep a smile on your face while you're talking. It may sound silly, but it works. Somehow that smile comes through and allows the person on the other end to feel comfortable with you. Make the person answering the phone an ally. End with something polite. "I'm looking forward to seeing Mr. Smith. My understanding is that the interview will be at four o'clock on Tuesday, June fifth, at 2335 Broadway on the third floor. Thank you very much."

IS THERE A WAY TO GET AROUND THE GATEKEEPER?

First of all, shift your approach: Don't try to get around the gatekeeper. It is more useful to try to get her help, and you can only do that by letting her know that you realize she is important. Gatekeepers shouldn't be regarded as simple message-takers for the people they work for—they are highly valued by the executives in their offices.

1. Act like you're happy to talk to the gatekeeper.

NO: "This is the third time you've told me she is in a meeting."

YES: "This is Michelle Sloan. If you could leave another message for Ms. X, I'd really appreciate it."

2. If the gatekeeper has told you her name:

NO: Thanks for your help, miss.

YES: Thanks for your time, Ellen.

If the gatekeeper has not offered her name, you may ask by saying something like "You've been very helpful. May I ask your name?" Courteous perseverance generally triumphs.

CHAPTER FIVE

SCOPING OUT THE COMPANY

NOW IT IS TIME to check out all those companies on your list. Some things you need to know are:

➤ What does the company do or sell to make money?
➤ How big is the company?
➤ How many employees work for the company?
➤ How does the company treat minorities?

ASK YOUR CASEWORKER, PAROLE OFFICER, OR A TEACHER TO CALL THE COMPANY. HE OR SHE SHOULD CALL AND GATHER INFORMATION BY PROMISING A MINORITY PERSON ON THE INSIDE NOT TO USE HIS OR HER NAME AND ANSWERS FOR ANYTHING OTHER THAN HELPING PEOPLE GET JOBS AND THEIR NAMES WILL BE KEPT UNDERCOVER.

Herdie Baisden, a black man, is vice president and general manager of Personnel Decisions International in Atlanta, Georgia. He suggests that African-American job hunters "check the ratings in *Black Enterprise* magazine" and get "the scoop" by talking to other blacks who work there. Latinos can check out Spanish-language newspapers and magazines such as *El Diario* and *Latina* magazine.

Another method is to go to your local library's research room and ask the librarian to show you how to do a search of newspapers and magazines. All you have to do is enter the company's name and you should get all of the articles written about the company over the past year. Read the articles. They will give you a lot of information that you can use to impress the interviewers.

Most cities have an organization called the Chamber of Commerce, which gathers information on the city's businesses. Through the Chamber of Commerce you can learn a lot about the firm that you are going to interview with. Ask the public relations representative:

➤ how long the firm has been doing business
➤ how many people the firm employs
➤ how many of those employees are minorities
➤ the names of the key executives

One last method of scoping out a company is to call the company and ask for its annual reports, which are available for free from most larger companies, and will tell you what the company does and how well it is doing financially. If you look at the pictures carefully, you can learn a lot about how the company feels about minorities. Look at the pictures: Are the people in the top jobs all white? All male?

CHAPTER SIX

MANAGING FIRST IMPRESSIONS

THERE IS AN OLD SAYING that "you never get a second chance to make a first impression." It is absolutely true. A great deal of how the interviewer remembers you occurs during the first five minutes after meeting you. You can gain many points by looking relaxed and focused on your goal. You can only look this way if you have all your bases covered and you know it. Here are the bases:

MAKE SURE YOU'RE WELL-GROOMED

The first base is cleanliness. If nothing else, make sure that you've just bathed before you left home and that your hair is clean and styled in a businesslike way.

Neat, close-cropped hair is usually preferred on men.

African-American and Latina women are advised to stay

away from the currently fashionable hair colors like blond and burgundy. Sure, you may look good in these colors, but if you are applying for work in an office, it can really startle an interviewer when a very dark-skinned woman walks in with platinum hair. You don't want to startle. You want to be treated as a skilled, professional person who would work well for the company. The same goes for makeup: Don't overdo it. Just a little foundation and lipstick is fine. And please, no two-inch fly girl nails with funky designs on them.

Men and women—don't forget the deodorant, and leave any other scent at home, even if you usually wear cologne or perfume, because the interviewer may not like or be allergic to the scent.

DRESS APPROPRIATELY

Men should wear a navy or dark gray suit with a white shirt, tie, and black dress shoes, no earrings or gold chains. If you don't own a suit, caseworkers or local church organizations might help you get one.

Women should also go for a smart, professional look. Wear a dark skirt suit (no pants), a white blouse, and flesh-colored stockings. This is not the time for sexiness, Don't wear big earrings and you can also leave the gold neck chains at home.

The look might be boring, but the goal here is not excitement. The goal is to become employed.

FEEL COMFORTABLE WITH THE WAY YOU LOOK

If you feel uncomfortable in your interview outfit, you will look uncomfortable. If you fidget, pull at your clothes, or nervously touch your hair, the interviewer will wonder what the problem is and start to feel uneasy, too. To get around this, dress up at least once in your interview outfit and get used to moving around, sitting, and talking in it.

KNOW HOW TO FIND THE PLACE

You don't want to arrive at the interview upset because you spent a half hour searching for the building. Unless the job interview is in a part of town that you know, do a practice run the day before the interview. This way you'll know which bus, subway, or driving route to take, and where to go once you start walking. Make your mistakes the day before the interview.

KNOW WHAT TO EXPECT

Once you arrive at the office, the receptionist will most likely give you an official application to fill out while you wait for the interviewer. After you're finished with the application, either the interviewer will come out or someone will show you to her office.

If the interviewer puts out a hand toward you, shake it pleasantly. Make sure your handshake is firm—neither too hard nor droopy. Wait until the interviewer asks you to have a seat before you sit down.

Now it is time for the interview to start!

CHAPTER SEVEN

BARRIER-BREAKING INTERVIEWS

YOU'VE DONE YOUR RESEARCH and found the right kind of company that offers the right kind of job. You've prepared a good résumé and mailed it with a cover letter to the company's contact person. You got a call from the company's receptionist to arrange an interview. You did everything right when you called back: You were polite, brief, you got the receptionist to tell you his or her name. You're dressed appropriately. You have another copy of your résumé just in case your interviewer does not have it handy. You're ready to land the job, right? Wrong.

Your job now is to gain the interviewer's respect with your skills, ambition, and knowledge of the company. The interviewer will try to find out just how truthful you are and how good a worker you are. Make sure you:

- come across as a nice, easygoing person.
- are clear about the skills you are offering.
- answer the interviewer's questions in an honest but professional manner.
- respond to both your and the interviewer's objectives and needs, not one or the other.
- listen intently to the interviewer.
- handle barrier issues and illegal questions related to race subtly, by using dialogue that will diffuse them.
- Change the employer's fear of the barrier issue into excitement about this new opportunity.

Even when people are prejudiced, they usually act as if they are well-intentioned. To win in a situation with a prejudiced person, be very positive, and give the person the benefit of the doubt. In other words, act as if they *are* genuinely well-intentioned. People who are the most positive in such situations tend to do well.

If you haven't rehearsed the interview, you are not prepared. It's hard to get hired in today's marketplace, and harder still if you face any barriers of race, ethnic heritage, or prior life history. Rehearsing the interview with a mentor or a friend who has solid workplace experience is a must.

ROLE-PLAYS FOR CREATING THE RIGHT FIRST IMPRESSION

You play the part of the interviewer and ask your friend or mentor to play your part. This is a chance to see how you look to the interviewer. Seat yourself at a table and ask your friend to leave the room and reenter it. Here's your opening script:

YOU/ INTERVIEWER [*standing*]:	Hello, Mr. or Ms. Name.
YOUR FRIEND/ INTERVIEWEE [*walks toward you and extends his hand to shake yours*]:	Hello, Mr. or Ms. Name. It's good to meet you. Thank you for inviting me to interview for the (job name) position here at (company name).
YOU/ INTERVIEWER [*shaking his hand*]:	Good to meet you. Have a seat.
YOUR FRIEND/ INTERVIEWEE [*taking a seat*]:	Thank you.

Stop here and evaluate your friend on the following:

➤ Warmth—was he friendly and approachable?

➤ Posture—did he stand up straight, hunch over, or carry himself arrogantly? Did he make and keep eye contact? Were his hands relaxed, or did he wring them or clasp the chair arm tightly?

➤ Speech—Did he pronounce his words clearly, or did he mumble or stammer? Did he speak too softly or too loudly? Did he use his hands to gently emphasize his words, or did he make wild, bold gestures?

➤ Handshake—Was his grip firm, limp, or just right?

Now, reverse the roles. I feel that the hiring decision is more often influenced by a great first impression than any other factor. Practice this scenario until you feel totally at ease with showing warmth, good posture, proper speech, and a winning handshake.

Next, reverse the roles again. This time you are an interviewer predisposed NOT to hire people like yourself. Here's your barrier-breaking script:

YOU/ INTERVIEWER [*sitting at a table/ desk*]:	Are you FirstName?
YOUR FRIEND/ INTERVIEWEE [*walks toward you and stands a few feet from the table/ desk, but not close enough to tower over you*]:	Yes, Mr. Name, I'm FirstName LastName. [*extends his hand to shake yours*] Hello.
YOU/ INTERVIEWER [*sitting at your table/desk, not rising or shaking hands*]:	Hi. Sit down.
YOUR FRIEND/ INTERVIEWEE:	Thank you. I appreciate the opportunity to interview for the (job name) position here at (company name).
YOU/ INTERVIEWER:	So, I don't have much time, and a lot of people already here in the company want the job.

YOUR FRIEND/ **INTERVIEWEE** [*taking a seat*]:	Thank you for taking the time. I'll briefly tell you the skills and abilities I would bring to the job.

Stop here and evaluate your friend on the following:

➤ Warmth—Was he even-tempered despite the poor treatment?
➤ Posture—Did he meet the seated interviewer by standing up straight, hunching over, or carrying himself arrogantly?
➤ Speech—Did he pronounce his words clearly, or did he mumble or stammer? Did he speak too softly or too loudly? Did he get flustered, hostile, or threatening?

Talk with your friend about how he felt in the situation. Chances are, those will be your feelings if you face a situation like this, or one with some of its elements. Talking through those feelings now will help you manage things, and possibly still get the job, should you face such an interviewer. In case you're asking yourself if you'd want a job where you faced such a person, the answer is yes. Often the interviewer is not the person you'd work directly with. Don't let a human resources preinterviewer, or a department head doing the hiring, keep you out of a job in which your direct supervisor might be a great person to work for. Learn how to break through the barriers in a thirty-minute interview to land a job that might change the course of your entire life.

Now, reverse the roles. Having played the hirer, you won't be overwhelmed by your feelings of anger or frustration. Manage your feelings as you practice overcoming barriers to create a great first impression. Ask your friend to rate you, and, more important, rate yourself using the evaluation list above.

PREPARING FOR COMMONLY ASKED INTERVIEW QUESTIONS—With your friend or mentor, review the following questions, and formulate your answer to each one, but do not write down the answers. It's important that you get comfortable with the content of your answers, so try not to remember the exact words you plan to say.

THE TEN MOST COMMONLY ASKED INTERVIEW QUESTIONS AND HOW NOT TO ANSWER IN BARRIER-BREAKING INTERVIEWS

1. **THAT** (weather, controversial topic in the newspaper, traffic, losing sports team, big political issue, etc.) **IS REALLY SOMETHING, ISN'T IT?**

    The interviewer is trying to break the ice, which is a good sign, but beware. Unprepared answers to such questions can make you appear negative or blaming, and can also lure you into barrier traps. "Yes, I hate this rain" or "You should've seen the traffic on Broadway" can lead to "Has weather affected your job attendance?" or "I guess traffic can make you late to work a lot."

    Do not exchange chitchat on any controversial topics— religion, politics, or otherwise—about which you could give a personal opinion. Instead, show that you are informed, and lead the conversation back to the job. For example, say, "I read about that, too. It's important to stay on top of issues in a job like [name the one you're applying for]."

2. **TELL ME ABOUT YOURSELF.** Many job-hunting books will tell you this is an impossible question, but it's a great one in a barrier-breaking situation because it allows you to present potential drawbacks in the most positive light possible. But if you're not careful, such questions can cause you to ramble and give the interviewer lots of information about you that is not pertinent to the job. Be careful not to give an answer of more than five points (list them in your mind) and make sure each one relates somehow to experience and skills you would bring to the job.

For example, point 1 might be "Well, I was born and raised here in Omaha, so I know the city well. That will help me learn the delivery routes quickly." Point 2 could be "I got my diploma from East High, and I know a few East High people work here. It would be good to be back with them; I'd be a good team player." Point 3 might be your barrier breaker: "You can see from my application that I made some choices I really regret. Since I've been back in Omaha I've been focused on helping other young men—I'm coaching some boys in the neighborhood on their basketball game, and [*easing into point 4*] on getting my work skills stronger. I've been temping as a delivery person for the past three months."

Point 5 might move on to more personal things: "I'm at the stage in my life where I want to commit. I know I'm ready to stick with a job like the one here at Ready Delivery."

3. **WHAT ARE THE STRONGEST AND WEAKEST THINGS ABOUT YOU?** In the best of situations, this is a game question designed to shake out any negative traits and to find out how introspective you are. In barrier situations, it's a trick question used to get ammunition to justify or rationalize not hiring you. In either case, do not give equal time to your weak points.

    In good situations, when you feel comfortable the interviewer is genuine, say something that turns your weakest point into a positive: "I am really compulsive—I like to get things done. If there's work to do, I like to do it right away." Then focus on your positives at length.

    Do the same in a barrier situation, but leave out "I'm really compulsive." Do not give the interviewer any information that might indicate weakness. Never let down your guard, and make sure to keep your story straight—do not say things that might sound contradictory. Express your weaknesses as strengths, since that's actually what they are. Our weaknesses are our biggest growth opportunities, so show how you've grown.

4. **TELL ME ABOUT YOUR JOB SEARCH.** Questions like this one and its more direct twin, "How long have you been looking?," are big barrier questions. They put you in a defensive position. Unless you have a job now and can

honestly say, "I've been looking for a long time, because I don't want to leave a good situation until I find a much better one," deflect this line of questioning. Do not answer it directly, and, if you have been looking for a long time, do not give reasons why. Instead, focus on why you are looking for this job. "I've been looking for a job like this one with (name of company) for a while because . . ."

5 AND 6. **HOW DID YOU GET ALONG WITH YOUR LAST SUPERVISOR? AND YOUR LAST COWORKERS?** Your immediate reaction is probably that the interviewer is trying to find out whether you pay attention to authority, and that is part of the question. The key purpose for this question is to scope out your social skills, how well you get along with people, and how well you fit on the work team. Do not react with arrogant disregard to authority or a phony docile submission to authority.

Talk about yourself as a team player. Describe how you relate to other players and how you relate to a coach. Your answer should talk about how you:

➤ boost others, and incite them to perform better.
➤ admit to and compensate for your mistakes.
➤ go along with the team majority or the coach—out of respect—even when you disagree with the play that's called.
➤ point out other team member's errors in a way that helps them do better without tearing their egos down.
➤ play fair and don't cheat, even when nobody would notice.

➤ keep an "up" and outgoing attitude even in difficult circumstances.

➤ want a victory for the team, not just an MVP for yourself.

7. MOST PEOPLE IN THIS JOB START WITH [SPECIFIC EDUCATIONAL ATTAINMENT] WHICH YOU DON'T HAVE. IS THIS [SPECIFIC EDUCATION YOU DO HAVE] REALLY THE SAME? Late in the interview, this question is a good sign: The interviewer has been persuaded to look for a way to fit you into the job criteria. Early in the interview, it may be a barrier question. In either case, do not say yes. You may lay the groundwork for having to prove to an irrational interviewer, for example, that a GED is the same as four years at an exclusive prep school. But do not say no, either, which can provide the irrational interviewer an excuse to end the session.

Instead, say, "Actually, a GED is better than a high school diploma for this job. While they are the same in terms of educational achievement, getting a GED requires more personal discipline and self-motivation than going to high school." Whatever educational standards you're being measured against, do not argue that you meet them if you do not. Do respectfully show that your level of learning parallels those standards and equips you better for this job than those set by the company. Believe your own words, because study after study has shown that people with life skills are more successful than people with book skills.

Show the interviewer that you are a lifelong learner who will continue to learn and grow on the job.

8. **WE ARE LOOKING FOR AN EXPERIENCED SO-AND-SO. YOU'VE NEVER DONE SUCH-AND-SUCH. HOW CAN WE HIRE YOU?** Again, at the beginning of the interview this is a tough barrier question, but near the end, it signals that the interviewer is looking for a way to justify taking a chance and giving you a shot at the job. Never say, "You have a point, but I know if I just had a break I know I would . . ."

If you sense it's a barrier, volley the question. Speak with all the confidence you have and firmly challenge the interviewer. "Oh, but I *have* done such-and-such. By raising four children—who are all in school, doing B+ or better work—on public assistance by myself, I actually have done clerical work. A clerk organizes and keeps track of things, and that's what I've been doing for fourteen years. And I do it very well."

If you feel the interviewer is on your side, give her the ammunition she needs to plead your case to her superiors when she advocates hiring you. Give her a laundry list. "I have been doing clerical work all my life, if you really look at it: feeding, clothing, and housing four kids on a public assistance check means I am good with budgets; they're all doing great in school, which doesn't happen if I don't keep up with their homework papers, so I am good at organization; raising kids is all about a million little things, so I'm really a detail-oriented person; each one has a distinctive personality, which proves that I know how to get along with all different types; you could look at my kids' report cards and see that I don't let anything slide—I pay attention to all of their school subjects, and I would do the same thing here for all the clerical tasks; I wouldn't have 'attitude' about doing things that aren't in my job description. 'Mother' might come with a job description, but 'single mother' sure doesn't."

9. **WHAT SALARY ARE YOU LOOKING FOR?** Do not give a number. The purpose of the interview is to land the job. The time to discuss salary is once a job offer has been extended. Say "I'm flexible" even if you aren't, and move on to proving that you are the right person for the job. "What interests me most about this job is the chance to use my skills . . ."

10. **WHERE WERE YOU BORN? YOU DON'T LOOK BLACK, ARE YOU MIXED? I SEE YOU HAVE ON THAT RING, ARE YOU A MUSLIM? GOSH, YOU'VE DONE A LOT IN YOUR LIFE, HOW OLD ARE YOU?** These questions are illegal. The Civil Rights Act is the national law that makes it a federal offense to ask such questions in an interview because the information gathered from them is not to be used in hiring. But you will probably be asked one of them, or something similar, at some point in your interviewing experience. Do not remind the questioner that the question is illegal. There are lots of good companies and good jobs that you might need to cross the barrier of a prejudiced person to get to, so don't allow one such person to block you. Reminding the interviewer that a

question is illegal may get you into legal proceedings, but it won't get you into the job you're interviewing for. But do not pretend the question isn't illegal. In some cases the interviewer is genuinely unaware of the illegality of his or her questions.

In either case, remain friendly and respond with confidence, as if you are giving the interviewer the benefit of the doubt by moving the interview back to relevant issues. "I'm not sure why that information is relevant, but I can assure you that my qualities [name them] are right for this job." If the illegal questioning is clearly intentional, you might pull out a notepad and say, "I wasn't prepared for such a personal line of questioning. I'm not sure what information you're looking for and why it would be relevant."

In many cases the interview questions are not the biggest barriers, but the reactions of the interviewer:

➤ Is this all the work experience you've had in your *whole* life?

➤ You were actually in jail? Is it as bad as they say?

➤ You have four kids and you've never been married?

➤ You mean they don't have real jobs on that island where you're from?

➤ Do other people have as hard a time as I am with understanding your accent?

➤ This job is going to be really hard for you. Are you sure you want to work here? I've been trying to get some diversity in this place but achieving diversity isn't easy, you know.

In every instance, let the interviewer talk until he or she has gotten over the shock, confusion, or whining. Listen patiently. Usually the person is not really looking for an answer and simply needs to blow off the emotion of the moment. Say "Mm-hm" or "Oh really." Offer an empathetic smile. These will go far in helping the interviewer calm down and get back on track. Then pick up with job-related issues as if nothing untoward had occurred.

Now you know how not to answer the questions, but how do you answer them? Be honest. Don't hide negatives from your past, but find the lessons in them. There is an old saying: "If it doesn't kill you, it'll make you stronger." How have your "barrier issues" made you stronger? What qualities and skills do you have as a result? Think about what's good about you, even ask your friends. Write the answers down. Are you loyal, organized, patient, compassionate, thorough, punctual, careful? These are attributes that make you employable. Find four such qualities and write them down. Now find a situation you can talk to an interviewer about that demonstrates each quality. Write it down next to the quality. As you answer the most commonly asked questions, use these qualities and situations in your responses.

ROLE-PLAYS FOR COMMONLY ASKED INTERVIEW QUESTIONS

After you have decided how you plan to answer each question, play the part of the interviewer and ask your friend or mentor to play your part. Ask the questions in the order you choose. Listen carefully to your friend/mentor's answers, and when you have completed the interview (asked all of the questions), evaluate your friend on the following points:

➤ Brief, to-the-point answers—Was your friend direct and clear without being too long-winded? Or did she seem vague?

➤ No excuses—Did your friend sound like a victim, or someone who can handle the curveballs life throws us?

➤ Honesty—Did your friend cover up negatives in her past work history, or address them in a straightforward, open manner?

➤ Explanations that took responsibility for and showed learning from past mistakes—When revealing uncomfortable matters relevant to employment, did your friend show that she had matured and grown? Did she make you believe she would not make those or similar mistakes again?

➤ Confidence—Was she comfortable with herself, not arrogant or passive?

Discuss your observations briefly with your friend, noting as you do that these are exactly the assessments your interviewer will make of you. Now reverse the roles.

Start from entering the room—repeating the first impression role play—and continue until your friend/mentor has asked you all the interview questions. Do not start over if you make a mistake. Just continue until the end. Ask your friend/mentor to evaluate you, and also honestly evaluate yourself, using the points listed above.

POINTERS ON ROLE-PLAYING

➤ LIMIT YOUR ROLE-PLAY PRACTICE TO NO MORE THAN ONE HOUR.
➤ REPEAT PRACTICE SESSIONS DAILY FOR THREE DAYS.
➤ SAVE CRITIQUES UNTIL THE END, RATHER THAN INTERRUPTING THE ROLE-PLAYS.
➤ ACT AS YOU ACTUALLY WOULD IN AN INTERVIEW DURING THE ROLE-PLAYS. DO NOT DOWNPLAY.

BARRIER-BREAKING INTERVIEW SUCCESS FROM REAL LIFE—A Care Manager at a major New York hospital relates these two experiences:

"At my last job, I hired a man who had several convictions for bank robbery. He had done federal time. He had a lot of things working against him: He was an alien; he did not have his GED; he was in his forties at the time. He had been fired from his previous job. But I advocated to hire him. The job was for treatment supervision. I used his liabilities in his favor. When hired, he worked there for four years and then moved on to another, better job. He showed in the interview that he was empathetic, had leadership qualities, and was a good listener—qualities that made him successful in the job. He spoke about how his life experience was relevant to the job's requirements. He showed sincere interest in the work. He was a very good listener in the interview. He asked concise questions, asking specifically what the job entailed. He volunteered himself for overtime, and only then asked if there *was* overtime. He was comfortable in the interview, his body was relaxed. He didn't appear nervous, and looked me in the eye. He thought about his answers before he spoke, not so long as to arouse suspicion that he was lying, but enough to show he was paying attention to what he said. From the beginning, he followed all the rules for a successful interview—he even waited until he was asked to sit.

"I also hired a woman who had been on public assistance all of her life. (She'd also been on drugs.) This was her first job ever. She was in her forties. I hired her as a counselor in a mother's program, where she is still working now, after two years. Her strengths are that she is compassionate, empathetic, and is able to hold people accountable.

"My advice to women is to speak as confidently as you can. Watch your hand movements. Don't cross your legs. (It looks like a sexual gesture.) No spiked heels, no short skirts, no flashy jewelry; wear sedate colors, only light makeup; make sure nails are neatly—not wildly—

manicured. Don't talk too much. Don't sound like a victim when you answer questions."

It can be done. Your past work and life history need not determine your future. In each of these real-life examples the interviewee showed how his or her life experience skills and abilities were right for the job. Each presented himself in a professional manner to the interviewer and, by doing so, won the interviewer's confidence. Neither hid his or her past, but neither dwelled on it. Again, they showed how they had gained key abilities and competencies from their past experiences.

The interviewer is hiring the person you are today. That first impression and how you handle the interview questions will mean more to many interviewers than what you did or didn't do in the past.

AT THE INTERVIEW—A SERIES OF FIRST IMPRESSIONS

You've completed your role-plays. The interview situation is no longer a mystery to you. You are prepared for the best and equipped to handle the worst. Now you are ready for that job-winning interview.

You've arrived a half hour to twenty minutes early for the interview. You walk to the reception desk: "Hello. I'm FirstName LastName. I'm here to see Mr./Ms. LastName for an interview."

If the receptionist is not overly busy or is particularly warm, and you were able to get her name, you might ask: "Are you Ms. LastName? You were so helpful to me when I called. Thank you." Be careful, if you are a man, not to appear flirtatious, and if you have any concern that such a remark might be construed as a "come-on," don't take the lead in opening such a conversation.

Believe it or not, the impression you make on the people you will likely meet before you get to the person with hiring authority is part of winning the job. People talk. When the interview is over and you've gone home, which of the following would you rather have said about you?

➤ The receptionist says to the hiring person's secretary at lunch: "That man who came in for the interview was the most polite candidate of all of them . . ."

➤ The human resources assistant says to the manager who preinterviewed you: "That guy who came in first thing this morning was pleasant. He got here early, but he was so patient while he waited for his interview."

➤ The secretary of the interviewer/hirer says to her boss after lunch: "Well, I hope you hire the guy who came in this morning. He fits in. Something about him made everyone feel relaxed."

"All of the above" is the right answer. Think of the interview as beginning the moment you arrive on the company's premises. Be polite and considerate to everyone you encounter. The skills of posture, speech, and warmth that you practiced in your role-plays are useful tools of interaction with everyone you meet.

THE BARRIER-BREAKING INTERVIEW

1. **ESTABLISH PERSONAL RAPPORT.** If you've rehearsed the first impression role-plays above, you're ready for the first—and most difficult—moments of the interview process. The role-plays allow you to make a favorable entrance without requiring your full concentration. Entering, greeting, the handshake, and being seated—should all be second nature, even if your interviewer presents initial barriers. As you enter the room, divide your attention between making that all-important first impression and finding a way to establish rapport.

    Rapport is established by finding a common experience and showing that you are not a threat. When you first walk in, find something in the office that you can relate to. Here's an example Herdie Baisden relates from his own experience:

    "I am a tall, large, dark-skinned black man. I am aware that my physical presence can intimidate. I went for an interview and sensed this from the interviewer right away. I noticed a Green Bay Packer helmet on a shelf in the interviewer's office and said, 'Hey, I'm a Packer backer.' That immediately made a connection with the interviewer and established rapport."

    You, the interviewee, have to make a connection with the interviewer. Yes, the barriers are of his or her making, but they are your obstacle. You have to break them down. Ignoring barriers or sulking through the interview will not make your interview a job-winning one.

Establishing rapport is essential, even for the most qualified candidate.

In the best situations, you will be able to establish a connection with the interviewer. In a situation where no eye contact is made, ask the interviewer a question about something in the room that will focus him or her on the object you are looking at. Or talk softer so the person has to look at you.

If the person isn't making any chitchat at all, act as if you realize the person is very busy, and ask gently, "What can I do to make sure that you get the information you need in the time we have for this interview?"

Even if the interviewer appears unwilling to make small talk or relate to you person-to-person, don't be discouraged. You may have scored a point just for trying.

2.   **LISTEN.** Once you've established or attempted to establish rapport, listen. Let the interviewer take the lead. As in the example of the ex-offender, listen carefully and thoughtfully to what the interviewer says and asks. You've prepared for the most commonly asked questions, but no two interviewers ask them exactly the same way. Make sure you understand what is being asked before you respond. Pause before answering to think about how you want to word your response.

If the interviewer talks at length about the job, listen carefully for the key information. Keep good eye contact. Show that you are receiving what the interviewer is saying.

3. **AVOID BARRIER PITS.** Most interviewers' barriers fall into two categories of expectations. They expect candidates like you to be defensive and have a victim mentality (that makes them feel blamed).

As the interviewer asks questions, listen for cues that indicate he or she thinks you've come to the interview with a chip on your shoulder or believing you won't get a fair shake. Counter such cues with optimism. Assure the interviewer that you are excited by the opportunities in the working world.

When asked about past job history or other concerns that may not be positive, talk openly about your weaknesses or shortcomings without giving excuses like "My boss did this or that." Instead of saying something like "Let me tell you about how I've been messed over in trying to move forward in my career . . . ," say, "I've learned a lot about patience and sticking to my guns even when it's tough, since I was fired from that job." Emphasize your positives: "What I've learned will help me get along with my supervisors. I always had perfect attendance; I only came to work late three times while I was there, and that was the year of the bus strike; and I volunteered for work beyond what employees in my position did."

Adopt the attitude that each person is an exception, and project it to the interviewer. Talk about how you have overcome obstacles, rather than the obstacles themselves. Avoid bringing up your particular "barrier issue" and certainly do not attribute any negative experiences to it.

If you can avoid falling into either of these barrier pits

in answering the interviewer's questions, you are well on your way to a barrier-breaking interview.

4. **HIGHLIGHT YOUR ACCOMPLISHMENTS.** When you can persuade the interviewer to focus on your accomplishments rather than the barriers, you are having a job-winning interview. Answer the interviewer's questions by sharing things you have done successfully. Even more than they want to see education and experience, interviewers want to hear about concrete, quantifiable successes. In your role-plays, you've practiced talking about skills and abilities you have learned outside the workplace that will make you successful in a job requiring those capabilities. Talk about them with confidence.

5. **END THE INTERVIEW PROPERLY.** Your interviewer will control when the interview ends. Listen for cues like "We'll get back to you" to let you know your time is drawing to an end, but do not rush out hurriedly. Let the interviewer rise from his or her seat first or tell you very specifically "Thank you for coming in" before you rise. Be sure to thank the interviewer for the opportunity and end with a warm handshake and eye contact.

As you leave the premises, don't forget to say polite good-byes to those who greeted you when you entered. The last impression is very important, too.

CHAPTER EIGHT

GOING FORWARD

AFTER THE INTERVIEW

As soon as you get home, write a thank-you letter to the interviewer. Here is a sample:

PATRICIA A. DANIELS
100 West 125th Street
New York, NY 10025
(212) 123-4567

June 3, 1999

Mr. Walter Gazek
Manager
ABC Insurance Company
1230 West 3rd Street
New York, NY 10004

Dear Mr. Gazek:

I am writing to thank you for seeing me yesterday in regard to the secretarial opening at ABC Insurance Company. It was especially useful to meet some of your other employees and tour the company to see how you work.

I am very interested in the position and look forward to hearing from you soon.

Thanks again for your time.

Sincerely yours,

Patricia A. Daniels

Wait at least a week after sending the thank-you letter. If you haven't heard anything from the company after seven business days have passed, you should call the person who interviewed you and politely ask if a decision has been made.

As soon as someone offers you a job, you should gently raise the issue of salary if he or she has not already done so. If you feel that the pay is too little, it is okay to say something like "Thank you for the offer. However, I do feel that in light of my excellent skills and background in _____ [*be sure your talents are outstanding and be very specific about them here*], the salary should be _____." Do not ask for more than $2,000 additional per year, and again, be sure you are worth it.

If the salary offered is okay with you, then simply accept the job by saying, "Thank you very much, Mr. or Ms. Doe. I look forward to working at _____ company. When do I start?"

GETTING READY TO ENTER THE WORKFORCE

Use the time before your start date to pull your work wardrobe together, gather the official documents you will need on your first day at work, and obtain enough carfare and lunch money to last until your first paycheck (usually at least two weeks from your start date).

THE NECESSARY DOCUMENTS—When you report for work the first day, bring:

- ➤ your social security card
- ➤ your birth certificate
- ➤ your green card (if you are an immigrant).

THE NECESSARY WARDROBE—A basic work wardrobe consists of the following:

MEN

- ➤ Black or brown dress shoes
- ➤ Dress slacks
- ➤ White long-sleeved dress shirts
- ➤ Ties

WOMEN

- ➤ Black pumps
- ➤ Dress skirts and blouses
- ➤ Conservative dresses (not tight, short, or revealing)
- ➤ Sheer pantyhose

KEEPING THE JOB YOU'VE WORKED SO HARD TO GET

You will be expected to have a basically good work ethic. This means several things:

- ➤ Show up for work every day—on time.
- ➤ Don't call in sick unless you are ill enough to see a doctor.
- ➤ Don't say negative things about the company to anyone.
- ➤ Don't talk badly about your boss to anyone.
- ➤ Get along with your coworkers.

➤ Be pleasant and courteous to everyone around you.

➤ Never lose your temper.

➤ Pay attention when someone is giving you directions.

➤ Don't make the same mistake twice.

➤ Pay attention to the company dress code.

Make sure you do a good job, keep your résumé up to date, and help the interviewer feel good about hiring you.

COMPANIES THAT HIRE EX-OFFENDERS, FORMER WELFARE RECIPIENTS, AND OTHERS WITH LITTLE WORK EXPERIENCE

Burger King Corporation—Nationwide

Cessna Aircraft—Wichita, KS

Faulkner Construction—Austin, TX

Gloucester Company—Franklin, MA

Goodwill Industries—Washington, DC

Marriott Hotels International—Nationwide

Microboard Processing—Seymour, CT

Mirage Resorts—Las Vegas, NV

Monsanto Company—Nationwide

Sprint Corporation—Nationwide

United Airlines—Nationwide

United Parcel Service—Nationwide

ORGANIZATIONS THAT OFFER FREE ASSISTANCE TO EX-OFFENDERS, FORMER WELFARE RECIPIENTS, AND OTHERS WITH LITTLE WORK EXPERIENCE:

AMERICA WORKS

575 8th Avenue, 14th floor
New York, NY 10018
(212) 244-5627

For people 18 or older and on public assistance. Children must be on the budget and in child care. Provides training in typing, computers, catering, and cashier work. Training lasts approximately six weeks. Week one covers career counseling, interview techniques, and reading and math skills. Students must be present every day or restart the course.

BEGIN PROGRAM @ BROOKLYN COLLEGE

80 Willoughby Street
Brooklyn, NY 11201
(718) 722-3446 or 722-3447

For people making the transition from welfare to work. Students receive GED; hands-on computer instruction in Windows, Word Perfect, Excel, and Print Shop; career counseling; support in job search and work experience.

BOTTOMLESS CLOSET

445 North Wells Street, Suite 301
Chicago, IL 60610
(312) 527-9664

Provides women who are referred through a job training program with two complete outfits for interviews. Provides career counseling skills, and after the woman is hired, Bottomless Closet will give her three more free outfits to wear on the job.

CAREER GEAR
424 Park Avenue South—Box 116
New York, NY 10016
(212) 252-4327

Provides men in need with a suit free of charge to wear on job interviews.

THE DOOR
555 Broome Street (2 blocks north of Canal Street)
New York, NY 10013
(212) 941-9090

For young people 12 to 20. Services include: GED and career counseling. Job placement for clients who are of age.

EX-OFFENDER SUPPORT GROUP—EMPOWERMENT PROGRAM
1245 East Colfax Avenue, #404
Denver, CO 80218
(303) 863-7817

For women who have been in prison or are currently on probation or parole and living in the metropolitan Denver area.

JOB CONNECTION TRAINING PROGRAM

This organization takes applicants at several locations in Florida:

Manatee Community Training Center
5512 Manatee Avenue West
Bradenton, FL 34209
(941) 795-0978

Sarasota Community Training Center
1540 Main Street
Sarasota, FL 34236
(941) 955-1339

Venice Community Training Center
1752 South Tamiami Trail
Venice, FL 34293
(941) 493-5077

Airport Community Training Center
7501 Bradenton Road
Sarasota, FL 34243
(941) 355-2721

PRIVATE INDUSTRY COUNCIL

17 Battery Place (near Battery Park)
New York, NY 10004
(212) 742-1000 (Ext. 352)

Offers educational training in business, air-conditioning and refrigeration repair, computers, English as a second language, GED preparation, on-the-job training. They have a "summer job for youth" program, and a youth competence program.

STRIVE
204 West 136th Street
New York, NY 10030
(212) 281-1200

STRIVE is a special service for adults 18–40 who want to improve their work attitudes and skills. If accepted, trainees attend a demanding workshop with strict work rules that prepare trainees for the real world of work.

WILDCAT SERVICE CORP.
161 Hudson Street (near Canal Street)
New York, NY 10013
(212) 219-9700

On-the-job training in a variety of jobs, including secretarial, catering, industrial, and manual labor.

ABOUT THE AUTHOR

ANITA DOREEN DIGGS is a member of the Authors Guild and the American Society of Journalists and Authors. She lives in New York City.